Heron Cliff

For Del,
with love,
Margo

2014

Heron Cliff

MARGO BUTTON

John Barton, Editor

Signature
EDITIONS

© 2007, Margo Button

Cover design by Terry Gallagher/Doowah Design.
Cover painting, *The Bird of Happiness*, by Carol Grigg.
Photo of Margo Button by John Yanyshyn.

This book was printed on Ancient Forest Friendly paper.
Printed and bound in Canada by Marquis Book Printing Inc.

We acknowledge the support of The Canada Council for the Arts and the Manitoba Arts Council for our publishing program.

Library and Archives Canada Cataloguing in Publication

Button, Margo
        Heron Cliff / Margo Button.

Poems.
ISBN 978-1-897109-17-5

        I. Title.

PS8553.U873H47 2007   C811'.54   C2007-902363-0

Signature Editions
P.O. Box 206, RPO Corydon, Winnipeg, Manitoba, R3M 3S7
www.signature-editions.com

for Natalie

"what death...? There is only
mine
or yours,
but the world
will be filled with the living."
                                    Franz Wright

CONTENTS

Heron Cliff

How many centuries before the spirit forgets the body?
How long will we feel our phantom skin buckling over rockface,
our pulse in magnetic lines of force?

Anne Michaels

HERON CLIFF

To plan is to let the gods preempt me again.

But what if, I say to my husband's dream
of moving to the city. *Why not?* he says
as he cracks open skylights, invites
the sudden nearness of birds.

Sixteen years ago we dreamed a house,
blasted granite, bulldozed earth, chain-sawed
Garry oaks and broadleaf maples,
drove off the kingfishers and flickers,
buried the wild lilies in a septic field,
altered the water table and killed
three old Douglas firs.

Blur of whirring wings.
Hummingbirds know
whose territory this is.

The cedar ceilings are pitched at every angle —
a rollercoaster of tree hearts laid bare.
In bed I count groove and tongue
instead of sheep, search for knots in clear wood
where no knots exist, discover
tidelines where there is no sea.

My friend paints the twisted fir
but the grass clumps
glowing at their roots
I've never noticed before.

What else have I missed?

—

Shriek of a juvenile eagle.
Shadow of his wings on the deck,
shadow of the adult following.

—

My mistake was thinking I owned this land
as if I had control over the roses
I cut to the quick, as if
they wouldn't flower anyway.

—

Friends wonder why I remain in a house
tainted by suicide. The long dance
I perform: allemande left, allemande right,
dos-à-dos with the dead.

—

The giant bonsai — shape of lightning rooted in rock —
leans out over the cliff, inviting westerlies
to prune it
and prune it some more.

—

Red tulips —
lipsticks, lollipops, paint pots,
goblets of ragged stars.

—

On the driveway a smudge of blood,
tufts of rabbit fur
caught like seeds in the *dents de lion.*

—

My son is a will-o'-the-wisp
at the back door enjoying a smoke,
in the kitchen brewing tea. Look, now
he's the cat's paw of wind on the sea.

—

On the seventh anniversary of his death
we throw daffodils and rhodo bells
into the waves, have a few words with him.

The dog turns his back on ceremony.
Nose to the breeze, he gathers other scents.

—

This spring the roses were devoured
by deer who walk the night
on this dead-end street teaching me
to do without.

—

A barnacle, I resist
being pried from home, though
daffodils trumpet spring elsewhere
and purple finches sing
songlines around other trees.

—

In Swedish legend, swallows hover
above the cross of the Lord, crying
"Svala! Svala!"— Console yourself!

Today they flash knives
above the steps where
my son sat down and died.

—

In the baby-blue-sea-and-mountain morning
Douglas firs are silhouettes
waiting for the sun
to give them substance.

—

Season upon season this landscape
overpaints me. No one
can scrape away the layers and
restore me to my land.

—

When we move house, can the past
be discarded like old furniture?

The steps where I found him dead.
The gazebo built in his memory.
The sea where he makes his bed.

—

I feel an urge to swat
the bright mobile
moon dangling in the crib
of the Garry oak.

—

At the window our two shadows
witness Mt. Baker hovering
above the sea a hundred miles away.
Leaving holds us here.

—

The eagle hunkers in the rain,
drenched feathers at a rakish tilt.
Home is any bare branch in a tall tree,
the more exposed the better.

—

Early morning, sea-light
trembling on the wall —
my son walks the house again.

—

Returning to earth, I'll praise the trees.
It won't matter if I'm in time or tune
or if anyone can hear. In the forest's heart,
to sing a song for the sake of singing
and not call it mine.

—

A cloud of clematis bloomed this week
without a sound.

Home Truths

...and what could be more comforting than to fold grief
like a blanket —
to fold anger like a blanket,
with neat corners —
to put them into a box of words?

Mary Oliver

THE FIRST WARNING

...the moment when we know ourselves to be unique, mortal, separate...
Bronwen Wallace, Common Magic

this is the house we live in
while Dad's away at war
the kitchen where Mother
herds us under the table
during summer thunderstorms
four of us huddled together
hanging on without a prayer

this is the snow fort I'm building
with my three-year-old sister
a towhead with a toy
wheelbarrow at her feet
a runaway smile on my face
our suits sticky with snow
from the roof just caved in

you are my sunshine
sings mother
my only sunshine
you make me happy
when skies are grey

this is the wood stove we cozy up to
among the clothes   scarecrows
with frozen arms and legs Mom lugs in
cursing wind and winter
and having to drag up three kids
on her own

please don't take my sunshine away

this is the day I get her goat
and she hits me with the poker
hard on my back   breaks the skin

like a lightning bolt expels me
into space where I circle
wary   unformed

this is the house where I begin
to stop loving my mother

HOME TRUTHS

Six of us in three rooms
above Dad's garage,
the baby in the pantry.
In this house of scrimp and save
Mom's homemade root beer —
stacked in the bathtub —
explodes during the night
and bottle caps pop everywhere.

Once, she and I tiptoe
into the rented offices next door —
she keeps a key in case of fire.
We leave the door ajar. *Shhh,
your father might hear.*

The open space is stark,
desks and empty chairs. Bare
windows look on the street.
Our footsteps echo
sticky on the green congoleum.

Pens, pencils, paper,
erasers she hands me. A fistful?
I'm not sure how many
or even how often she stole
but guilt is an indelible ink.

At any moment, heavy boots
may thump up the stairs —
my soft-spoken, slow-moving dad.

No one will miss a few things.
Was that her excuse?
Or was I?

FACING THE MUSIC

My singing teacher, a white-coiffed lady,
somewhat deaf, is pure
United Empire Loyalist
and lives in a Georgian brick home.
After the lesson she lends me her opera book:
Take care. Gold letters, avocado brocade
I carry home feeling the heft of it, the responsibility —
the first book I've seen
as grand as the family Bible.

In my bedroom I turn the pages
gingerly. Here are all the libretti
I've scribbled in haste from the radio
every *Saturday at the Met.*
The first time I've seen the divas:
etchings of Renata Tebaldi, the buxom
soprano as Desdemona.
Here, the set of *Aida* at La Scala:
real elephants lumbering across the stage.

And then, Valkyrie on a warhorse
                    — my mother
swoops into the room, girded for battle,
shouting *fortissimo* so the neighbours hear
I am no help at all stuck upstairs, a *prima donna*
with my nose in a damned book again.

Flung from the window
it lands on the driveway — spine broken,
pages soiled. The svelte
coloratura, Lily Pons can shatter
crystal when she hits
high F.

While eight identical windows stare
in wide-eyed judgment, I slip
the book inside the teacher's storm door,
close it softly

    and bolt.

DIAMOND IN THE ROUGH

Imagine me in that stupid school uniform —
seventeen-year-old daddy-long-legs
in black stockings and short tunic.

Every morning is a battle royal.
Evenings I retreat to moon over Elvis.
Who loves me tender, loves me sweet?

My handsome airman in Mexico,
thirty-six hours by Greyhound.
I've got my solitaire and
I'll be on the bus soon as I save enough.

After school I work for Jack in the jewellery store,
dust crystal, sell rhinestones, worry about
being cross-eyed and perspiring too much.

There's Jack at his bench repairing a watch,
bald head gleaming under a gooseneck lamp,
loupe fixed to his glasses — a goggle-eyed fish
who surfaces too quickly when customers come in.

Selling diamonds is Jack's department —
rose-cut, teardrop, brilliant with fifty-eight facets
he dips in cyanide, polishes till they catch fire.

Diamonds are stars. Look at them in the light.
Some burn blue, some yellow or red —
the colours come from impurities.
Mine are the best in town, no flaws at all.

How those huge hands replace an escape wheel
or solder gold claws on a ring
is hard to figure. But that Billy Bass mouth
sure can talk, and he talks and he talks
until he talks me right out of eloping.

AS SHE SLIPS OUT OF HER SEASONS

He's in hospital
but she thinks he's left her
for another woman. In the window

pane, a stranger looks back —
stone eyes, cobweb hair. On the street
maple trees loosen their leaves

in loops and curls like family photos
coming unstuck on her wall.
Where have all the hydrangeas gone,

the juice and joy of roses? She forgets that
gardens have their own come and go.
The haute couture of summer —

how stylish she once was —
has been reduced to the dry leaf
clatter of fall and muffled birds.

SHE HATED BEING REFERRED TO AS "SHE"

So demeaning, she said, like a thing
that doesn't own a name.
After the hearse collected her body
Dad and I sat for hours in the backyard
philosophizing beside the tuberous begonias
and marigolds he'd planted
so she'd see them from her sickbed.

He told me about the robins' nest
she'd watched all spring. Did I want
an open casket for her? I did.
He didn't. How hard it was, he said,
choosing a dress to bury her in
(the ugly purple one she hated).

Like a squirming child, I dove and swam
through that long underwater afternoon,
surfacing once in a while to chase bubbles
bursting inside me, my body reckless,
knowing what I dare not admit:
I had Dad to myself at last.

I longed to make bitter yellow garlands —
as festive as they are in India.
I longed to drape them
from the mailbox and maple tree.

HOW STILL MY FATHER

In the bedroom, he stands stock-still
listening to a flock of crows —
psychopomps cawing from the garden shade.
Hand to chest, he coddles the knot of his heart.
That large blue hand I've seen
in some surrealist painting near a stopwatch.
Its numbers stretch and slide.

On the wall hangs a photo of Chamcook Lake
where he hunted deer with his brothers.
He aimed a .30-30 through the trees
one fall and shot a stranger
by accident, a bullet in the arm.
The screams stopped Dad in his tracks
like a deer — bewildered, wounded —
a second before his heart bolted in his chest

as it did just now
while I was spreading a comforter on his bed —
an early Christmas present he might as well enjoy.
You've had a good long life,
I say, preparing myself for the day
he steps into the dappled trees and disappears.

IN HIS EIGHTIES HE USED TO SAY
HE WAS LIKE AN OLD CAR

The mechanics dismantle an old Jag engine
shiny as a stainless steel basin.
Two surgeons pass wrenches back and forth,
loosen bolts, expose pistons and valves,
the greasy camshaft. Hands smeared black,
they syringe out the sludge and talk about how
the Poms used to wire every part in place,
what masters they were at casting engine blocks.
The Yanks, in a rush to get cars off the assembly line,
never built one as good.

I'm at home with gas and grease,
pungent smells of my dad's garage
where I dropped in on the way to school to scrounge
a dime for a Roy Rogers comic or a bag of dulse.
At the entrance to the dark sanctum I'd wait
until he surfaced from the grease pit
where he'd been cleaning a carburetor
or changing a gasket. Wiping his hands
he'd exit into the light, pinch my earlobe
with a grin. He was telling a story
about hunting partridge with his brothers
or the Model A he bought in 1940,
the one that fell apart all at once.

DAD

Four old electric razors
     1936 marriage certificate
          World War II medals

RCAF brass buttons
     Twenty-five jackets
          Three drawers of socks

A bag of golf tees — half broken
     A photo with a python around his neck
          A talking fish called Big Mouth Billy

Deeds for every house he'd owned
     Three putting machines
          A phone message the night before he died

This is your dad   Hope you're all happy

WHILE A STUFFED HEART ROASTS IN THE OVEN

A sunny winter day in 1919
my grandmother sits down in the farm kitchen,
writes a letter to her sister

while George is down for his nap —
such a nuisance, this new baby.
Roger and Edward are at school.
Ernest,
> *Anna*
>> *and Gordon*
are outside sliding down the hill
towards the ice-covered brook. Any minute,
they'll be at the door — icy hands, rosy-apple cheeks
— stomping snow on my clean floor.
This week, I made pocket-pants for the boys,
a dress for Anna from an old flannel middy.
I barely have energy to turn
the mangle and churn…

Time crayons over our family tree,
muddles generations, the indelible
order/disorder of our lives.
She is young again
and I am old, filled with her future —
Not very newsy, she writes.

Roger will plunge over the cliff in a car,
drown in the Ottawa River.
My son will die at the same age as hers.

So we sit a while
together at the scarred oak table, savouring
the smell of stuffed heart,
listening for the baby,
the stomp of boots at the door.

TRIBUNAL PLACES BLAME ON TRAIN 118

1

My grandfather was a name
I heard as a child. A blurry photo
you kept beside your bed
for thirty years, Gram, long after
you must have forgotten his touch.
His eyes were obscured by a Panama brim.
A gold watch and chain dangling from his pocket —
twenty-five years as a CPR engineer.

2

January 7, 1936, a wintry day in Maine,
he grabs his lunch pail, rushes off
to the yards, signs his daily orders:

> *Train 3745 —*
> *twenty-six cars of grain and logs —*
> *are heading your way*
> *at ten miles an hour.*

> *Train 118 —*
> *pull off at Lowelltown*
> *until they pass.*

He swings into the cab of 118, lumbers down
the sharp grade —
he knows every tie in that road.
The crew is busy stoking
the passengers' coal stove, writing custom reports.

Too late, they realize he's overrun
the switch, accelerating

around the bend. No time
to reach the airbrake. He's trapped

on those rails, struggling
against all odds, unable to
sprout wings. Like Houdini, escape
his steel straitjacket.

3

Train 3745 and Train 118 collide
at 10:15. Exactly.

  Where were you, Gram, at 10:15?
  Did you wonder how
  you could *not* have known?

Screeching brakes drown
  the men's screams. Steam geysers.
    Logs are pick-up sticks
      hurtling through the air.

The engines crumple
like accordions and topple.

He is crushed.

A fireman is trapped in the cab. Another,
pinned under burning logs,
hollers, *My God, boys,*
you're not going to let me burn alive!

while bystanders, helpless,
throw snow on the roof.

4

In your eighties you confide
he used to call you "his little lobster."
That suit of armour, those nasty pincers.

Silly, I think. Green or red?
Alive or cooked?

Who was he, Gram, before
the family buried him for his mistake?
Did he wave at children waving at crossings?
Was he dazzled by sunrise glazing the rails?

What was on his mind that morning
he came back to kiss you again?

MARGINALIA

for my great-grandmother

Margaret left me a book without a cover
by Henry W. Longfellow,
which I bound in marbled paper
and blue leather stamped in gold.

On the flyleaf she'd scribbled her name
embedded in her husband's:

Mrs. James McDowell
St. Andrews, New Brunswick
April 20th, 1909.

I never knew her but
there she is tucked among the poems —
white bonnet of hair, eyes lost
in shade. Her shapeless black dress
conceals the crucible of
seven children,
seventeen grandchildren.
This seat of trial,
this used-up belly she clamps
with root-like hands.

I search for a whiff of her
on the page: a turned-down corner,
a smudge by her favourite poem,
but all is must, untouched
like ecru gowns crumpled in mothballs
forgotten in a trunk. A bit of muslin,
they called women
when she was young.

WE WERE GOING TO THE ORPHANAGE ON BUSINESS

Maybe, we told our son —
floating the idea — we might find
a little girl there looking for a family.

When she didn't appear at dinner
he started crying —

> our husky twelve-year-old,
> the karate wannabe
> who used to wait behind the door,
> jump out at us
> like Tarzan on a gazunga.

Yes, he wanted a sister.
Oh course, he did.

> RANDALL, I used to scream
> when he disappeared at dinnertime.
> RANDALL, the parrot shrieked
> loud but not loud enough
> to wake the dead.

> I'd start laughing and
> the parrot would mimic,
> so I laughed even more.
> That house was bedlam.

Then Andrea moved in
trailing giggles
like bubbles behind her
and he changed his mind.

ON THE SEVENTH ANNIVERSARY OF MY SON'S DEATH

I meet a baby
with a quizzical crimp in his forehead.
Two new-minted eyes
gaze at me the way
my baby gazed a lifetime ago.

He jerks his puppet feet,
whap-whaps my face
with dimpled hands —
a mechanical bear
inviting me into the toy store.

Hey, lighten up, lady,
the little guy says
with a two-tooth grin.
I'm the world's baby.
My mother is
the mother of millions.

NATALIE MARGARET

Elfin ears, ragamuffin hair, chestnut eyes wide as a deer's.

Kitten tongue slips in and out over the rough edge of her first tooth.

Today she learns to turn her head sideways

for a different view of the world.

Today I practice with her.

SO THIS IS HOW GRIEF ENDS

There are days when I long
for his children who never were.

     I grab Tom by the seat of his pants
     as he leans over the brook
     throwing bread to the ducks,
     squealing when they catch it.
     A bite for Tom,
     a bite for the ducks,
     a bite for Molly the dog.

     Eight-year-old Sara, the foster child,
     wants to write a poem
     for her deaf mother who has
     something wrong with her head.

     Searching for eels, Bobby wades
     down the brook, adrift from us
     in her autistic world.
     Last week at the circus
     we rode a rickety car
     through the Haunted House
     where she covered her ears
     to keep out the screams.

These small rushes of love.

Reconnaissance Mission

For Randall (1967-1994)

NO TRADE-INS ALLOWED

I bought, you bought a

Tsimshian mask of a human
transforming into an eagle

> The winter we accused our son of
> using drugs, he reproached us
> for having possessions

Thai Buddha with mother-of-pearl eyes

> He shaved his head and in monk's dress
> meditated among the wild rhododendrons

Oxford red leather Bible
that lacked ingredients tasty for worms

> Euphoric, he communed with God, blamed us
> for not sending him to church as a child

Wool rug from Beijing
ancient coins woven dead centre

> He sold his gold chain and the ring
> engraved with his Chinese name
> but nothing drove away his demons

Gilt carving of soldiers on horseback
from a home ransacked by Red Guards

> One night in a back alley, he wrestled
> his father to the ground, stole his wallet

Balinese kris, its bloody history
embodied in the blade

      He ripped off the hilt, pawned
      the ebony lion with ruby eyes

Floppy clown dressed in red hearts
from close to home

When he was diagnosed we tried
to strike a deal with God.

NEIGHBOURS IN BIR HASSAN

Beirut, 1973

The machine-gun bullet left a ragged hole
the span of a hand
ripping through the curtain,
imploding in the living-room wall.

We awoke on the battlefield —
our chests — amplifiers reverberating,
volume turned too high —
to jagged rhythms of mortars and Kalashnikovs.

> Lebanese in armoured cars
> surrounded our apartment block,
> Palestinian guerrillas holed up
> in the stadium across the street
> though we didn't know

that night we rushed into the living room,
entranced by flares soaring past the windows,
hovering, soaring, hovering.

> My husband crawled about on marble floors
> eliminating targets —
> lamps we'd just turned on.

> *My knees were sore for days.*

Neighbours' shouts echoed in the stairwell.
Our six-year-old in my arms,
I raced down seven flights of stairs.

> *Where were you? I looked everywhere.*

In the basement the concierge
pointed the way to a bomb shelter
we didn't know was there —

a cement chamber with steel door,
no windows, a dirty toilet
for nine families.

One neighbour slipped upstairs, grabbed
a shaker of vodka martinis,
Valium, blankets, a radio —

the newscaster knew less than we did
(and diplomatic immunity
wasn't worth a damn).

The khamsin blew that night —
the hot Saharan wind that carries sand
and burns your eyes with grit.
We curled up like animals, hot bodies
spooned together on the cement floor —
my husband, son, the maid and me.

    Overhead, morning thunder of jets.
    Whoosh and thud of rockets.

When the pandemonium bled into silence
we climbed into the car, everyone
hunkered down but the driver,
foot to the floor as he headed for town.

    Out of ammunition, the Palestinians
    retreated to their shanties in Bir Hassan,
    to their sloe-eyed women
    and kids who played in the mud.

    Every Christmas we'd driven into
    that refugee camp near us
    though we never spoke to anyone, just drove in,
    dropped a turkey and a big bag of rice
    in the middle of the road
    and backed out again.

AT THE COTTAGE

Listening for my ten-year-old, calling out
as he swam in the lake below
I used to sit on the balcony weaving odds
and ends of sleek silk, knobby wool.
At Lac Notre Dame
every landscape was possible.

Sugar maples and white birch cloaked me
in shifting patterns
while my son scoured the shore for crayfish
and bright stones he brought to enrich
the tapestry. Penelope at her loom, I
wove the ins and outs of our lives while

mournful loons would wake us at dawn.
Autumn came: a canoe trailing
skeins of mustard, russet and crimson.
Across the ice wolves howled winter:
snowflakes spinning, the tortured
black trunk of a cedar.

Years later who could imagine this boy —
now a man who still loved to swim —
would swear he'd once seen Queen Victoria
underwater streaming towards him
in black veil and gown.

SOMEBODY'S PLAYTHING

When the boy yanks the starter cord
the inflatable boat leaps up — a bronco
bucking him into the chop —
and takes off full throttle. The boy,
his life jacket on board, dangles
in the saltchuck a hundred yards from shore,
flounders as his boat hurtles past
again and again — a snarling hellhound
encircling him while you
stand, helpless, on shore.

The engine slows to a purr
and you hope it will stall, but no,
it revs and takes another run at him,
so close —

an orca toying with a seal.

The prop slashes his jean jacket,
the flesh underneath. He wails
and all you can do is shout,

"Swim!"

ONE CRY

Hot Water Beach, New Zealand

From the cliff house, I hear a siren,
watch a rescue team scurry across the sand
to a cluster of people
out of their element: no one swims,
no one lies in the sun.
They stand in twos or threes,
stick figures on shore
still as white-faced herons.

I close my curtains but can't stop watching
the drowning — a sneak preview
of the end. I cosy up to
someone else's death.

One day in Mexico I saw a yacht explode
— swirling flames in the bay,
black smoke unreeling a silent movie,
no actors in sight.
Boats circled the pyre until
it slipped into a seamless
grave. I am witness again

but this time, a cry keens around the cove,
vibrates in me like a tuning fork.

As the stretcher is borne along the beach
a woman staggers and falls behind,
the body going on without her.

WORD COMES FROM HOME
OF A YOUNG COUSIN DYING

Tata Beach, New Zealand

We saunter along the beach
    settle on a rough bench

thigh to thigh
    allow clouds to tow us

across sea and sand
    where fig marigolds stretch

their blind-man's fingers
    and red-beaked gulls

squabble over scraps.
    Flung up by last night's gale

a few scallops gape.
    Why these we ask

and not others?

THE EMPEROR GUM MOTH

False eyes on its furry wings
stare down predators.

Pink scales shade to brown, overlap
like a cloak of quetzal feathers

sewn for an Incan emperor
who once sat on a throne

sipping bitter cacao, the drink of kings.
But the moth has no mouth.

What artist painted the finishing
touch, a dab of white —

light glancing off the dark pupil
to make it real? Why bother

about such a tiny life
hobbled from the start?

LOS DESAPARECIDOS

1

GUATEMALA, 1979

Market day in Chichicastenango,
a Mayan woman sits in the plaza
weaving a huipil
on a back-strap loom, one end
around her waist, the other
anchored to a tree.
With a baby planted at her side,
she gives birth to hibiscus, double-headed
bluebirds, parrots, quetzals in
colores alegres. Legends
woven along zigzag paths
may be snakes or lightning.
All directions intersect at the neckline.
In the highlands, a woman is
her village. You know her home
by the design
she slips over her head.

2

The women stopped weaving, stopped
wearing huipiles. Patterns identified them
as targets for terrorists
during the civil war.

Old women died, old ways
were forgotten.

3

GUATEMALA, 2003

Anthropologists are excavating
a mass grave in Paxcabal.

A crone recounts how two decades ago
the military assaulted
the villagers. Accused them
of harbouring rebels,
padlocked the men in the schoolhouse,
torched the village. The women and children
melted into the hills,
resurfaced among the ashes.

Today their high cheekbones are
trowelled clean by grief, by knowing
not knowing who lies
buried under the avocado tree.

A fingerbone unearthed, a toe, a series of ribs —
the scientist dusts them off
until a whole skeleton appears,
scraps of a stained shirt, a tooled leather belt
a woman identifies. She climbs down
into the grave, whimpering
her son's name.

HIS LAST CHRISTMAS

We're just sitting down to dinner —
his place looming at the table —
when a collect call comes from Eugene, Oregon.
He's cashed his welfare cheque,
hopped a plane with a girl he just met,
a will-o'-the-wisp he followed home for the holidays.
East Indian, Mom, so lovely but
there are devils at her house with white shining eyes.
He wants to come home but he's lost
his money and ID. *Don't worry about me;*
Sally Ann food is good this time of year.

We wire a bus ticket.
A friend will vouch for him at the border.
Grandpa says, *You'd have to be crazy*
to go to the States these days,
the exchange rate the way it is.

Boxing Day, 5:15 am, he phones to say
he's hitched a ride to Samantha Falls.
Girls still on his mind — he means
Klamath Falls, two hundred miles farther south.
Don't disappear, Randall. Please.

How we used to laugh at his antics,
the time he set off the fire alarm in Grade One
and emptied the school, the time

he ran away from home to the end of the block.
Don't disappear. Please.

RECONNAISSANCE MISSION

for David Smith Jr.

1

They criss-crossed the skies of Europe,
young guys doing dogfights
in million-dollar Sabres,
pretend-enemies in a make-believe war.

Forty years later, my husband and Jim
recall their drinking days: the squadron mascot —
a wild boar someone let loose on the air base —
the Iroquois cuts the boys got
before going to gunnery school in Sardinia.

We had to be cock roosters, says Jim,
in order to survive. I'll never forget that day
returning from a low-level sortie,
just 900 feet off the deck. I turned around and
Dave Smith, my wingman, was missing.
So I spiralled up, flew back,
found a pillar of smoke, nothing but the tail
with crossed tomahawks
sticking out of the ground.
Reckon he died from negative Gs,
poor bugger. And his wife, five months pregnant.

The fighter pilots climbed into their cockpits,
invincible again. Dave,
"the pilot who died young" —
became an epic that grew in the telling.

2

Dave was my *wingman,* my husband said.
(He'd been telling the story for years.)
Jim was flying somewhere else that day;
he only imagined it happened to him.

3

We scrimmage with death
but the dead belong to us all.
I took my son's life
and made his story mine, described
a hero — pale and partial

chimera of who he really was, a body
of words skewed to fit
my need to form him again
and again from the glad beginnings.

He became "the son who died young"
because I dwelt on his end.
Every word I would select a theft
obscuring how alive he had been
If he could call me
to account, I'd reply,
Who were you then?
Did I only imagine you happened?

THEY INVITE THEIR FRIENDS
AND THEIR FRIENDS' FRIENDS TOO

Of the 5,000 best-known human genes, 75%
have matches in the worm.

A dozen roundworms could perch
on a pinhead. Spirits
swaying to a ghostly hymn.

Yet they eat, defecate,
give birth and die, more like us
than angels with outlandish wings.

So many hearts, yet spineless
and blind. The worm's-eye
view is humble, yet

beware as it turns.
The bait we impale
will have its revenge.

GARDENER TEAPOTS

Sept. 12, 2001

This morning the sun rises alizarin crimson —
juice pressed from the madder root.
I take my favourite porcelain mug —
stencilled with an English country garden —
and while the water boils
add a pinch of Russian Caravan
to the tiny pot with the cracked lid.

> Gardener teapots —
> red, yellow, blue bone
> china — made in Russia
> under Peter the Great,
> lugged by camel caravans
> over the Silk Road to Pakistan.

Waiting for the tea to steep, I hear
the great blue heron's *kraak*
as it lumbers into flight

— birds in the air, fish in the sea,
and the world did not end
yesterday in New York.

> When the pots broke,
> menders salvaged the jagged bits,
> bound them with copper lugs
> and sealed the cracks with tar
> so they could again brew tea.

SKY-CALLING

for Ron

The albatross has a wingspan twice as wide as you are tall
and hollow bones so light

she barely moves her wings in flight, those long thin wings
hinged to fold like an origami bird

though she stumbles on earth with big webbed feet —
a gooney in floppy shoes.

Every winter she circumnavigates Antarctica, buffeted by icy currents
and Katabatic winds,

lands on the ocean only to feed and rest — though how she sleeps
in avalanches of water

is a mystery to me. Once a year she returns to breed
on the Tairoa cliffs,

flapping her wings in a hullabaloo, craning her neck to the sky
and screeching for her mate

until he comes and sits by her side, as if to say,
I need you. I'll always need you.

Blue Dahlias

To die in life is to become life
The wind stops skirting you
And enters. All the roses, suddenly,
Are blooming in your skull.

Rumi

BLUE DAHLIAS

A celebration of life seems appropriate. For the living at least.
We search tidal pools for starfish, anemones, our reflections.

Death camas swath the park in blue. My thin friend sits in the sun
in long sleeves and wide hat. One round of chemo to go.

Seeds drop on my head. Grey squirrels take risks playing
snakes and ladders in the elms. Nobody wins.

Of the dead I loved, there is only one death — yours.
One date etched in acid.

Before the parade, children wait on the curb for clowns.
A moving van (U Pak Only Once) follows the hearse.

—

We made 70,000 decisions building this house.
Whatever. We must do something while waiting to die.

Where is the owl who lived among the Garry oaks,
the sky's snarled threads?

A tent caterpillar crawls down his arm. The only welcome
wagon in this neighbourhood.

For hours the vizsla sits by the pool watching the koi.
Katina's marina.

The lost-purse dreams have stopped. I searched every city.
And for what? Mating robins and loudmouth crows.

—

Black bamboo and rosa rugosa provide privacy in the new garden.
"Eats Shoots and Leaves" or "Eats, Shoots, and Leaves"?

Though we shredded the fabric of this land
the bushtits weave themselves back in.

Water cascades off the wood sprite's hands.
Natalie trundles around the house emptying drawers.

Each plant is located according to the garden design.
Sprinting after squirrels, Katina snaps off the peonies.

Memories are plastic bags over my head.
Suicide in that house of rock and fog.

—

The kid says I'm too old for rollerblades. The sign:
"Drive slow. Watch out for rugrats and old biddies. "

You're only given a little madness. You mustn't lose it.
Those brown eyes. That smile. I'm in love!

The big bruiser orders me to move my car
parked in front of his house. Says he's a cop.

So? I'm a poet. A raging granny too.
It beats depression or medication.

We've made something beautiful. Why apologize?
I'm old enough to stand up to bullies.

—

The heron's beak points next door but her jaundiced eye
focuses on the koi pond. I'm keeping count.

Chasing barn swallows, the dog's in her glory.
In the Yuchi language God is a verb

and there is no word for temptation.
Birdfeeders hang from the eaves beyond reach.

Grief / weighs down the see-saw; / joy cannot budge it.
I do not subscribe to this. Cannot.

The dog explodes into motion, a racehorse
out of the gates, exuberant as a springbok.

—

Tent caterpillars burst with a pop, spraying
the sandstone rust and lime. I have no mercy.

In the yard, the music of bronzed Greek gods
with rippling muscles. Play at work, work at play.

I'm feeling *déracinée* while new plants take root.
Will the gardeners ever leave? And the turquoise port-a-potty?

At the club an oak tree fell, demolished three cars.
In summer there's no warning. And in winter?

Natalie picks up their weightless bodies, mesmerized
as they curl around her fingers.

—

The dog brings home a finch
throbbing in her loose soft mouth. No harm meant.

After the upheaval of moving, the soul requires
months to catch up. Dig earth, pull weeds, feed birds.

White spots on the caterpillars' heads are fly eggs.
Don't kill those. Remember the Jains.

Swoosh. Two mallards skid onto the pond,
rise on struts, fan and shower. Welcome.

Rhodos in tarty dress, plain-Jane grasses,
crone oaks rigid with vines. Everyone gathers.

—

Teenagers speak "up-talk." In a world hostage to terror
everything is in question.

Bateman couldn't wait for the lichen to grow
so he painted some on the rock face.

Each morning robins sing praise *ad nauseum.*
The Maori elder was grateful for a good BM.

A dream crone appears with a yellow caterpillar
wriggling from her nose. Thou shalt not...

So many words are endangered. In Boro,
onguboy: to love from the heart.

Natalie is a monkey grasping my trunk.
When you got up this morning how did you avoid

thinking about death? The kildeer skitters
across the grass distracting us from her nest.

Every act has my fingerprint. Are these stone walls
safeguard or prison? Or simply stonewalling?

The way is through gratitude. Dogwood blossoms
tinged with pink. Three fawns playing tag.

Why cower under blankets?
Baby's tears spread among the flagstones.

—

In this house toys are required, not *objets d'art.*
Poets should be poor and lead simple lives.

How to describe the dance each tree performs?
The wind choreographs such abandon.

There's the cleaning and polishing, the insurance,
the alarm system, the misgivings. All that weight.

The linden is threadbare, every leaf veined and
mottled like an old woman's hands. Yet precious...

the ragged sunspots it pours on stone.
In this garden dread must not take root.

—

According to Zen, one must learn the spirit — *kokoro* —
of each plant and rock before placing it in the garden.

I treasure the copy of Molière's *Comédies*, published in 1760.
Doesn't mean it's valuable, said the antiquarian.

Magnolia grandiflora, clematis alpina, camellia japonica.
Why this obsession for naming?

Imagine a language where *you* is the first person
and one feels uncomfortable saying *I*.

The bushtits' nest is a sock of cobwebs, moss and lichen.
Sit in the woods, wait for the day's offerings.

—

Whose dilemma is this? A birddog lives here
and two mallards are guests.

On a rampage, Natalie pulls apart the blankie
she calls *mama*. The air electric with screams.

The basalt flagstones are so massive, we call
the woodland path the Appian Way.

No need to go on wandering. A frog comes
racheting under the full moon.

Only three stumps remain of towering elms
that embraced our family farmhouse.

—

Walking the path we perfume the air with mint.
This landscape we create together.

Gold coins glisten as koi knife the water
slurping pellets in their pursed mouths.

Such a foofaraw today when *mama* had to be washed.
Injustice depends on one's point of view.

The architect finds the rooster vane flimsy
for a concrete roof. Now the wind blows wherever.

I covet this verb from the Boro language:
mokhrob —- to express anger with a sidelong glance.

—

Longing — a whirling dervish — gathers me
in its relentless skirts.

Natalie has discovered her ears but Katina's long flaps
are a puzzle. The sun shines through them!

Onsra — to love for the last time. Tears lie in wait.
Lie in state. O Randall, my phantom son.

The old farmhouse looked forlorn
so my sister painted the elms back in.

Let the earth lie lightly on you. Thus,
Romans bade their dead goodbye.

—

Three babies due in the family. A bumper year
for strawberries, poppies, caterpillars.

The kinnikinnick was devoured to feed a multitude.
Our universe is in flux.

Spiders erected scaffolding on the Appian Way.
Now they're wrapping up the house.

Where is my madness hiding? Too shy
to make the leap? Who ever dances now?

In Jaru, to be wise is to have ears.
How delightful her gibberish!

—

Resurrecting the dead is pathetic!
The dead are dead. Dead. Stone dead.

Inuit remain comfortable with long silences.
Ice and snow are their teachers.

Let's be silly, build a spirit house in the woods
where Natalie can drop off messages for fairies.

To dance like helixes of water-light
playing on the cedar ceiling!

New words on the tip of her tongue
ready to leap and dive. Then who will she be?

—

What patience the artist displayed:
a lifetime of trees one dab at a time.

Why not describe weather by the way
it feels on the body? Forget about degrees.

Try to get inside the infant's vast wordlessness,
which is the same as the silence of a teacher.

Elms descend to keep us company,
sprouting leaves thick as fur along their trunks.

I phoned Pacific Blinds
but wanted Illuminations.

—

Heart pounds on the dark's door. Too much
red wine. Blood grass in the shade.

We create each other. Who am I without him?
A reflection? An idea? Breath?

Halleluja! No brazen deer tiptoe around here.
Only a brass gazelle under the dogwood.

At first light, anxiety slinks in, a sticky customer
searching for something to adhere to.

Flick-flock of fountain, trickle of birdsong.
Forget weeds for a while.

—

The neighbour pats my dog— a random act
worth noting as I gather kindness.

Cedar waxwings — aflame — flash back and forth.
Oak branches die *after* they crash.

Let's plant forget-me-nots and bleeding hearts
while koi splash among the parrot feathers.

Rock-a-bye baby on the treetop. Natalie falls,
drowns in a dream-pond. She has no words.

The heron's body in flight — delicate blue
stamen of the paradise-bird flower.

—

Weather, a second skin. Hot auburn fur,
fog-moist arms, wind-battered face.

Those old nightmares of losing my boy —
they came true.

Blackberry lolls over the property line.
Musky privet too. Thorny, pesky neighbours

Now if I could erase this splendid sorrow,
would I?

Natalie's busy tongue darts in and out.
She spends too much time with dogs.

—

I interrupt a moonsnail, its foot plunging a clam.
Egg cases like inner tubes half-buried in sand.

The toddler plunks down beside a stranger, offers
a fistful of sand.

Fog everywhere, nowhere. Harrumphing
bullfrog-foghorns. Houses painted *sfumato*.

Jellyfish are lenses casting self-images in the sea.
The old lady complains about her new corneas.

A friend pities me for being a slave to objects.
Just an observation.

How to forget childhood's flashbulb memories?
The cod with a kitten in its stomach.

The drowned fisherman,
a starfish glommed to his face.

That 200-year-old yew is rather elderly
to fan dance in the wind. Yippee!

Desire-lines in the garden coincide
with the paths laid down for us.

Who'd guess that yews once haunted graveyards
and hung out with dead Druids?

At the golf club old ladies tsk-tsk as a bare-belly
teenager walks by. I'd better mind my p's and q's.

She described her friend as "a kick in the head."
It was meant as a compliment.

In the Zeballos courtroom the slain girl's relatives
and the killer's embraced.

School's out. Teenagers parade the beach.
Were we ever so beautiful?

This seems significant. On Dallas Road
I know the dogs' names but not their owners'.

—

Why call a flower "impatiens"
when it waits all winter to bloom?

Phantom of the opera —
the diva with laryngitis mouthed her arias.

Those picky Oak Bay juncos tossed aside our seeds.
Raindrops chainlink on the pond.

My 80-year-old friend bursts into song. "Up, up I go,
said Froggy. I can climb as well as hop."

"Sister Thérèse" at my feet —
a pious hydrangea! Strait-lacey.

—

Naming may be a waste of time. According to the Tao
the nameless is the beginning of heaven and earth.

My dreams have flatlined. Now where?
Four fledgling barn swallows confer on the grass.

At times, the moonsnail must leave its shell
or suffocate. Katina digs a hole to China.

Same old pond round and round.
They don't even swim upstream!

Wild track — kids whoop next door.
A friend on Saltspring bought two donkeys.

—

At the FolkFest an Indian gentleman sang
ghazals. How serendipitous for me!

Talking to strangers I discover friends of friends
but lose my tongue with a man who dislikes birds.

The Japanese maple dances a tango in red
on the water. Koi slap their tails.

Those rejected birdseeds are sprouting under the feeder.
Natalie wings stones into the pond.

Stupid to cry over what is not. You at twelve
with brooding look, a parrot on your shoulder.

—

We have no gate. Only entrance pillars.
Does a house need a name like a baby or dog?

The history of weather inscribed on trees —
lightning gashes, phantom limbs, fallen leaves.

When the doctor diagnosed terminal cancer
the crone danced. What you must fear is not to have lived.

Katina is one sexy babe gob-smacking,
lickety-splitting every dog in the park.

Ivy's embrace strangles the oak. The velcro
grandmother brought a suitcase of baby clothes.

—

Compliments on the new house and garden
become tedious, have nothing to do with...

The sudden magic of "Hi," a throwaway word,
her first. Doors open.

Caterpillars gone, the Camperdown elm
recovers its good nature.

So he reminds me
to be loving. Why be ashamed?

The granite erratic was streeled here by a glacier.
One way or another, we're all transplants.

—

Upended, a spider crab is comical
brandishing pincers like boxing gloves.

The nuthatch couples stick close to home.
Yet they don't know their name.

Christmas in July. The yew decked out in rubies.
Edmontonians shovelling hailstones.

It's too hot to view Art in the Street.
Let's enjoy what's on our wall.

Forty-two years married. In his anecdotage
he spins stories of his other selves.

—

Purple finch. What a misnomer!
What do finches call us?

June Callwood said that dying was easy compared to
losing a son. She'd already made the journey.

The Society labels schizophrenics
consumers! What do they consume but themselves?

The painted woman has blank eyes with no pupils.
Black lips too. An avatar I want to forget.

Snow on the lawn —
Katina has disembowelled her green moose.

—

A hot dry summer.   The oaks are crotchety.
We too shall be pruned and culled.

Give away the owl collection.
Too many eyes, too many hangers-on.

Why label the lavatera? It's enough
that pink blossoms sprawl in all directions.

We've swapped a million gene fragments. In a lifetime
we've become each other!

The crow exploded on the transformer.
A murder of crows gathered.

—

A hoe, a spade, a rake — what more do I need?
Gardening is an instrument of grace.

Ordinary delights grow here — barren wort,
bugbane, fountain grass, meadow rue.

And maybe, one day, blue dahlias —
something rare, unheard of.

Why build a fancy house when you desire a cottage?
Travel doesn't satisfy craving. Craving for what?

Dervishes whirl around their hearts,
burn like a torch. This too is prayer.

—

A friend sends a weathering —
haiku to hang on the Japanese maple.

Katina suns among the lavender. Nose tweaking
the breeze. Not a cloud in her eyes.

Slug-bitten, the drooping hydrangea plays
the drama queen. Drink to me only.

We are your gardens dying, blossoming.
Naming does not destroy the mystery.

I wander the garden looking for poetry
under the bushes. We play cat and mouse.

—

Harvest moon shines through the stained-glass sun.
Tonight the heron is fishing.

Sly weeds huddle close to flowers they resemble.
I pulled up hostas by mistake.

The caress of lake water
like butter, velours, a forgotten lover.

When a winning racehorse dies, they bury its head, hooves
and heart. In a race the heart makes the difference.

Katina disappears in white caps chasing gulls out to sea.
Natalie toddles next door to visit the man with Alzheimer's.

—

I imagine myself in picture hat and long gown
snipping flowers in the garden. Incorrigible romantic.

A chickadee gets trapped in the skylight.
The only escape: to move away from the light.

Sometimes, by mistake, we call the baby Katina.
Neither animal seems to mind.

After receiving a venomous email, I dream
of floundering through ice water up to my knees.

Ancient Chinese sent a sketch of a bamboo leaf
to indicate all was well.

—

That scruffy squirrel plucks fluff from her tail
to build a nest. The perfect little homebody.

Natalie touches my eye, nose, mouth as if naming me.
A startling intimacy.

A man dies after eating monkshood. Keep an eye on
those two behind the bench; they're no longer innocent.

House finches skirmish at the feeder, oblivious of
Katina's yellow eyes tracking wasps.

My father's haunt is a comforting companion.
But not yours. You died a stranger, my son.

—

This garden is an aristocrat with good bones:
mature elms and oaks, granite outcrops. Flesh of flowers.

Ancestors speak more kindly than the Bible.
Nor do they label women virgins or whores.

Slanting rain scribbles out the trees, the shed.
Ancient beaches come to life in the sandstone.

I — who heard your first cry —
how did I miss your last? How?

Remember when you discovered puddles and
autumn leaves? Why did you stop singing?

—

On the window a downy smudge of grey.
Lucky bird had no inkling of death.

Now you have a namesake, Randall.
This time, Fate, please be merciful.

But his mother, my niece, is stone deaf.
How on earth will she hear his cries?

Don't talk to me of another dream house.
In a nightmare it stood empty and dark.

I've photographed her a hundred times.
Afraid she'll disappear?

—

Mimosa folds its serrated leaves when touched.
The way that woman embraces — shrinking.

Stressed by drought, oak limbs *pop off.* Acorns
pelt the roofs. We're besieged!

I have an encyclopedic memory for slights,
most of them imaginary.

The rhodo is tricked into a second blooming
as summer, the harlequin, shrugs off.

Little dervish whirls, circles within circles —
concentric thoughts. Until she falls.

—

And a baby was born without bladder,
anus and penis. How sacred is life?

Awake or asleep, strangers surround me.
Even my self, a stranger.

Why read incessantly of other lives?
My sight is failing, my hearing too.

I yearn for landscapes reduced to essentials.
The Arctic. The desert. The soul.

Newborns resemble their fathers. To assure their survival,
claims my daughter.

—

The Chinese symbol for poetry is composed of
"word" and "temple." Am I a priest then?

The resident squirrel feasts on yew berries,
Fuller Brush tail flicking off raindrops.

Grandpa forgot to wind the grandfather clock.
Hurry up! A downy woodpecker's at the feeder.

Yapping like a jackal, Katina circles a one-eyed gull
with broken wing. We return it to the sea

and walk away from squawking crows.
Franz Hals painted two hundred shades of black.

—

Those tragic operas I wallowed in as a kid —
I should have gone skating instead.

Clothes are one obsession I neglect to mention.
As if poets are above all that.

Rain on the fountain. First time in months
the water sprite's back and bum are wet.

May each couplet be a *bouchée*, a petit four,
an *apéritif* to whet the appetite.

Jagged flashes in the corner of my eyes.
Captions in comics. ZAP, VROOM, WOW.

—

In Haida Gwaii, aboriginal houses had names:
The Something Terrible Happened House.

House the Clouds Sound Against as They Roll
Upon It. Ahhh! Listening to clouds.

Lost joys: dancing, swimming, skiing.
So! You're not dead yet!

How fearless the young. My niece plans
a water birth. No painkillers.

The little attic room waits with empty arms
for grandchildren to embrace it.

—

Katina is vociferous when we embrace.
Wedges her way between. The other woman.

Yes, you goofy dog, those acorns dropping on the roof
could be squirrels.

We sold the Something Terrible Happened House
without telling the buyers what. Happened.

Being a sinner isn't all bad.
You think twice about judging others.

Now I live in Cascades — a house without memory,
named for stone and tumbling stream.

—

She appreciates openness. The cleansing power
of rain and a friend who offers ground cover.

Imagine a heart: the size of a handful of
earth. Hearth. Heart.

The Big Wet has arrived. Despite their acrid scent
it seems brutal to pull up geraniums. Their stillborn buds.

Vultures — headless, tilting like drunks —
muster for the flight across Juan de Fuca Strait.

Dogwood is a corruption of daggerwood
used to make spears and arrows.

The same vultures we saw
riding thermals in Puerto Vallarta.

That pastel was perfect because it *was* unfinished.
Everything sketched in. But the face!

If a glass of red wine is good for the health,
surely three are better.

4:00 am. Focus on shifting light inside the eyelids.
A cave woman watching a dying fire.

When arranging flowers, leave enough space for
butterflies to flit through.

Empty spots in the garden are full of promise
like a stack of new white canvasses.

This is good therapy: snorting like a pig
with my head in a plastic bucket!

The finch left a tail feather in the living room —
scalloped brown with a coral shaft.

Acorns like ball bearings underfoot. He crash-
lands on the street, embarassed, bare-assed.

To sing like Kiri Te Kanawa! The mercy
in her voice like a melting candle.

—

Startled at the goat's bleating, Natalie draws back.
Everyday astonishments.

Oh for a crystal ball to look in on lost friends and lovers!
Old voyeur, what difference would it make?

The trees — *how simply they let ...fall the riches of a season,*
how without grief.

Though they're wooden and ache,
why be angry at my fingers? They're me.

The davidia waits ten years to produce souls or handkerchiefs,
whatever you call the blooms.

—

The first day that sunlight shimmers
on the kitchen ceiling. Earth turns.

Cobwebs in the house's armpits. The spider labours
to repair the filaments I destroyed.

Early morning, both sun and moon are on duty.
Her teenage son fell through a canvas roof and died.

Walked the bad-ass dog to stop her staring.
Brought the sensitive plant in out of the cold.

I've become a student of light. Clotted cream
on the shed. Molten gold on a dying cedar.

—

Berserk crows heckle a Cooper's hawk.
Dining at Chateau Victoria we argue about panhandlers.

All fears boil down to one: dying.
Terrorists know this.

We argue if a friend has a good quality of life.
Maybe we should ask *him*.

The green moose is replaced by a python
with a red felt tongue. In the scheme of things...

Love implies longing implies suffering.
I am too lazy to escape the vortex.

—

Japanese secretaries are "office flowers."
Lasting one season? There for the picking?

The sun's white eye. At the tideline,
orange sunflower stars washed up overnight.

The dog stalks out the door, pointing at phantoms.
Can't be too careful, Grandpa used to say.

I walk the earth in big gumboots, trample
the unsuspecting. By what right?

You would have been thirty-seven today.
How to measure a season against the calendar of your absence?

On the driveway: chestnuts ground to paste,
scritching leaves, mashed yew berries.

A great blue heron drops in for Thanksgiving.
Koi for dinner.

Don't bring white anemones indoors —
moon spirits may not be friendly.

God help us! Jesusland rules the world!
Fortunately, we live in the outposts of empire.

Acting the grandee, the barred owl strolls by the pond.
Aware of the honour it bestows?

Horsefeathers, like blue dahlias,
are hard to find.

Air-dried heirloom tomatoes on the gourmet menu.
Who dares eat them?

I teach Natalie the word "umbrella."
She starts pounding her chest like a gorilla.

At Halloween the lion cub learns to roar
but refuses to put on her head.

Look in the blank eyes of Modigliani's women.
Or a Haida mask. Each soul a sphinx.

—

I don't miss the old house or the phantom
who resides offshore — residue of a son.

Sluggish koi lull themselves into winter
slumber, falling asleep in snow.

On the bench a pumpkin lurks
longing for a face.

Poor woodpecker flew off, leaving tail feathers
in your hand. The scrunched leaf crouches on edge.

I do miss the spindrift/spoondrift. The seal with her pup
in spring, the harlequin regatta, the eavesdropping rain.

—

Millefiori: daffodils, tulips, hyacinths
put to bed in the dark wet earth.

I want to be gentle in old age like an autumn leaf
swooping down to meet the ground.

Natalie calls me Namu (Nana).
I feel like an Inuk.

The alphabet soup you spoke was preferable
to your black-cloaked silence.

The dog vibrates from snout to tail. Beside herself,
yiping all the way to the beach. To be so alive!

—

If I would dance like a leaf, I must
push the air and let the air push me back.

The rich woman was arrested for poisoning
five trees in the park. They obstructed her view.

Some neighbours delighted in her misfortune —
schadenfreude. Let's steal this word!

A downpour ignites a flock of chickadees
and my elderly friend who walks in snow, sleet, wind.

One October evening a devilish red moon in eclipse
distracted everyone on the navel-gazing earth.

—

The artist has gathered 30,000 leaves. Preserved,
numbered and inscribed each one with poetry.

She used this project *not to deconstruct,*
criticize, or satirize, but to know.

Natalie asleep in my arms. The order of my universe
no longer reversed.

It cannot be denied: I've become a dried apple doll.
And my poem: a ratatouille.

Physicists have reduced the chaotic dance of a falling leaf
to three lines of equations. What the bleep!

—

Shorn trees stretch their skeletons.
No burden of nests till spring.

Surrender to fear — the lurking hyena —
and it skulks away.

In a foggy envelope the chestnut trees stand expectant,
stock-still. He waits for his biopsy results.

At the garage sale what relief to see your old clothes
disappear down the street. Sold for a dollar or two.

Listen to her sobs, her small sorrows
as keen as ours.

—

She knows her comforts: a blanket,
a bottle, a hug.

Dim Sum means "to touch the heart."
I prefer something intangible.

The menu in Puerto Vallarta offered
jam omelette and *overflew brains*.

Fear diminishes, steals my words, my sleep.
Yet makes me more loving.

This week we welcomed the heron, the owl and the hawk —
the home we've been longing for.

NOTES

The epigraphs throughout the book are taken from the following: *Walking to Martha's Vineyard* by Franz Wright (New York: Alfred A Knopf, 2004); *Fugitive Pieces* (Toronto, M&S, 1996) by Anne Michaels; *The Leaf and the Cloud* by Mary Oliver (Cambridge, Mass: Da Capo Press, 2000); *Common Magic* by Bronwen Wallace (Ottawa: Oberon, 1985); and *The Soul of Rumi* (San Francisco: Harper San Francisco, 2001), edited by Coleman Barks.

"Heron Cliff"
"Leaving holds us here" is taken from *Leaving Holds Me Here* (Saskatoon: Thistledown, 2001) by Glen Sorestad.

"Los Desaparecidos"
huipil(es): short poncho worn by Mayan women.

"Blue Dahlias"
"You're only given a little madness. You mustn't lose it.": Robin Williams in an interview.

Yuchi is spoken by American Indians of the Creek Nation while Jaru is an Australian aboriginal langue. Bora is spoken in northeastern India and surrounding countries. All references to endangered languages are taken from *Spoken Here* (Toronto: Random House, 2003) by Mark Abley. The following quotations are also drawn from Abley: "Imagine a language where you is the first person and one feels uncomfortable saying I," "I covet this verb from the Boro language: *mokhrob* — to express anger with a sidelong glance," and "*Onsra* — to love for the last time" (from the Boro language).

"Grief / weighs down the see-saw; / joy cannot budge it." is from "Tubes" in *Old and New Poems* (Boston: Houghton Mifflin, 1990) by Donald Hall.

"When you got up this morning how did you avoid thinking about death?" is attributed to Spalding Gray in *Double Somersaults* (London: Brick, 1999) by Marlene Cookshaw.

"Let the earth lie lightly on you" is taken from *Dante in Love* by Harriet Rubin (London: Simon & Schuster, 2005)

"Try to get inside the infant's vast wordlessness/ which is the same as the silence of a teacher" and "We are your gardens dying, blossoming" are taken from *The Soul of Rumi* (San Francisco: Harper San Francisco, 2001), edited by Coleman Barks.

"When a winning race horse dies, they bury its head, hooves/and heart. In a race the heart makes the difference." is quoted from *Long Quiet Highway* by Natalie Goldberg (New York: Bantam, 1994).

"We create each other" is taken from Hegel.

"Weather, a second skin "appears in *Hannah and the Holy Fire* (Lantzville: Oolichan, 2003) by K. Louise Schmidt.

"What you must fear is not to have lived": June Callwood in a *Globe and Mail* interview, July 2004.

"Gardening is an instrument of grace," "…like a stack of new white canvasses," and "how simply they let … fall the riches of a season, how without grief" are taken from *Journal of a Solitude* (New York: Norton, 1973) by May Sarton.

"Cobwebs in the house's armpits…": *The Shape of the Journey, New and Collected Poems* (Port Townsend, Copper Canyon, 1998) by Jim Harrison.

"How to measure a season against the calendar of your absence?": *The Time in Between* (Toronto, McClelland & Stewart, 2005) by David Bergen.

"…not to deconstruct, or criticize, or satirize, but to know": *Hundreds and Thousands,* an exhibition by artist Diana Thompson (Surrey Art Gallery pamphlet).

ACKNOWLEDGMENTS

Several poems have appeared previously, sometimes in slightly different forms, in the following publications: *Event, The Fiddlehead, Room of Our Own, The Malahat Review, Arc, Takahe* (New Zealand), and *Poetry New Zealand* as well as the chapbook *The Invention of Birds* and anthologies: *The Cut* (NZ) and *Let it Go: Poems and Stories about Loss* (editor Hugh MacDonald).

A shorter version of "Blue Dahlias" co-won *The Malahat Review*'s Long Poem Prize in 2005. It was also the featured poem of the day on the *Poetry Daily* website and won the gold medal for poetry in the 2005 National Magazine Awards. The present version, with minor differences, was published as a chapbook by Leaf Press in 2006.

"Heron Cliff" won honourable mention in *This Magazine*'s The Great Canadian Literary Hunt in 2005.

Warm appreciation to my friends, the Island Poets, for their tough editing, generous spirit and wisdom.

To Marlene Cookshaw for editing my manuscript even though she was unwell, to Brian Bartlett, my cousin, for his sensitive and thorough editing, and to John Barton for shaping and refining the book.

To Ron for his ongoing love and support.